THE MESOLITHIC PERIOD

THE FIRST HUMANS AND
EARLY CIVILIZATIONS

THE MESOLITHIC PERIOD

Lori Fromowitz

ROSEN
PUBLISHING®

New York

Published in 2017 by The Rosen Publishing Group, Inc.
29 East 21st Street, New York, NY 10010

First Edition

Library of Congress Cataloging-in-Publication Data

Names: Fromowitz, Lori, author.
Title: The Mesolithic period / Lori Fromowitz.
Description: First edition. | New York : Rosen Publishing, 2017. | Series:
  The first humans and early civilizations | Includes bibliographical
  references and index.
Identifiers: LCCN 2015050846| ISBN 9781499463118 (library bound) | ISBN
  9781499463125 (pbk.) | ISBN 9781499463101 (6-pack)
Subjects: LCSH: Mesolithic period—Juvenile literature. | Prehistoric
  peoples—Juvenile literature.
Classification: LCC GN773 .F76 2017 | DDC 930.1/3—dc23
LC record available at http://lccn.loc.gov/2015050846

Manufactured in China

CONTENTS

INTRODUCTION

The earth warmed. The Ice Age came to an end, bringing change to the planet. As glaciers melted into the sea, the ocean waters rose. They flooded the land. In some places, land where humans had lived was now buried underwater. Much of the continent of Asia was submerged, leaving behind islands surrounded by sea. The Bering Land Bridge, which once connected Asia to North America, was also submerged, leaving the two continents separated by the Pacific Ocean. Britain separated from Europe and became an island.

In some places, the rains increased. The Sahara, today a dry desert, was likely filled with lush green vegetation after the ice melted. In northern Europe, the ice finished melting about ten thousand years ago. This was later than other parts of the earth, and the change brought about swifter and more drastic environmental change. What was once frozen tundra filled with dense forest populated with new species of plants and animals.

The end of the Ice Age in Europe marked the beginning of a new period, called the Mesolithic period. The Mesolithic period was between the Paleolithic, or Early Stone Age, and the Neolithic, or New Stone Age. The Mesolithic (*meso* means "middle," while *lith* means "stone") was a short period, lasting a little

This life-size diorama of people living during the Mesolithic period is at the Musée de Préhistoire des Gorges du Verdon, a museum in Quinson, France.

more than five thousand years in Europe. It took place between the end of the Ice Age and the beginning of farming and settled civilization.

In Europe, the Mesolithic began with the last glacial melting, roughly around 9000 BCE and lasted until approximately 3000 BCE, depending on the location. This is approximately five thousand years prior to today. In part because the ice finished melting at different times throughout the earth, the term "Mesolithic" does not mean the same thing in all places. In fact, many archaeologists use the term only in reference to northern Europe, which experienced a drastic climate change in a short period of time; the people therefore went through big cultural change in a brief period.

The term "Mesolithic" is sometimes applied to indicate the time following the melting ice elsewhere, too. In particular, it is given to archaeological sites where deposits of microliths, or small stone tools, are found. Examples of such tools are found throughout the world, including in Europe, Africa, the Middle East, Australia, and the Americas. In parts of Africa, microliths had been used for at least twenty thousand years before their use in Europe.

There is much we don't know about the Mesolithic period, and researchers continue to develop a picture of this time. They do know that Mesolithic period people were nomadic hunter-gatherers. They used the resources of their new environment and continued to develop the stone tools first used in the Paleolithic to adapt to their changing earth.

CHAPTER 1
THE MICROLITH AND MESOLITHIC TOOLS

What happened to all of the cave art? During the Paleolithic, people painted striking images on the walls of caves. The famous Lascaux Caves in France and the Cave of Altamira in Spain are from this period. The pictures tell archaeologists a story of what life was like for Paleolithic people. Around the time that the ice melted, the artists seem to have suddenly vanished. We have found very little cave art from the Mesolithic period. Perhaps, think researchers, the people making the art moved away. As the ice retreated, maybe many people had left Europe, too.

There is another puzzling problem, though. Small stone tools were found scattered throughout sites in Europe. These tools could be dated to the Mesolithic period. The tiny tools do not seem as powerful as the larger stone tools of the Paleolithic. Nor are they as polished as the stone tools of the Neolithic. Why did tools become seemingly less powerful during the Mesolithic? Shouldn't technology have continued to get better over time?

The lack of archaeological materials from the European Mesolithic period suggested to researchers that the Mesolithic in Europe was a dark age, or a period of decline for humans. People did not know how to respond to the changing climate and new world. They retreated, or perhaps they simply waited out this difficult time without advancing. Eventually, interaction with people from other places introduced the changes that brought the Neolithic Revolution. Until recent times, the Mesolithic was seen as a gap between the long Paleolithic and the big changes of the Neolithic Revolution.

Over time, more Mesolithic archaeological sites have been unearthed in Europe and in other parts of the world. A new picture of the Mesolithic period has emerged—not of an empty gap or a period of decline, but a period of transition. The humans of the Mesolithic period demonstrated flexible adaptations to a changing climate and the new world around them. Their adaptations helped to bring about a new, settled way of life that led to modern civilization.

The best evidence for this period of adaptation is in the tiny tools that Mesolithic people left behind. These microliths are proof of how humans learned to survive in a changing world.

MICROLITHS

The microliths of the Mesolithic were small, carefully shaped flakes of rock. People made them by striking flakes of stone off of a cone-shaped core. These cores were small and portable—ideal for hunter-gatherers who were on the move. Microliths of different shapes

These microliths with pointed tips were found at the Star Carr archaeological site in North Yorkshire, England.

can be dated to different periods or cultures of the Mesolithic. The small tools are often found in shapes such as triangles, trapezoids, rhombuses, and crescents. Archaeologists use these shapes to determine when the tools were made.

Like the tools of the Paleolithic, microliths were typically made of flint. Flint is a hard sedimentary rock. It is easily flaked, or chipped off, and can be used to create a sharp blade. Flint was often readily available and easy to work with. Mesolithic people broke flint from the surface nodules, or bumps, of the rock chalk.

Flint was not the only rock used to form microliths, though. Tools were made from whatever natural resources were available in a particular region. In the Alps, a range of mountains in Europe, Mesolithic people sometimes formed microliths out of rock crystal. This is a clear quartz crystal that has many of the same properties as flint rock. The shiny black rock obsidian and the colorful mineral jasper were also used to form these tiny tools.

The evidence suggests that Mesolithic stone workers became quite skilled at making microliths.

Archaeologists have found areas that were devoted to the making of these tiny tools. The finely crafted tools of the Mesolithic era were the result of practice over time.

TOOLS OF ADAPTATION

Microliths may have been lighter and less sturdy than larger stone tools of the Paleolithic, but they had other advantages. They could be used for new and more diverse tasks. The hunter-gatherers who lived during the Mesolithic period were adapting to changes in their environment, particularly in Europe. These small blades were a reflection of the changing world. In the Paleolithic age, the people had hunted large animals or animals that lived in herds. They could use large stones and overpower the animals through force. Mesolithic peoples now hunted smaller animals. This new prey required clever planning and quick thinking.

Microliths were easily portable. It was easy to quickly switch from using a microlith for one task to using it for another. After all, Mesolithic hunters may have needed to hunt an animal in one moment and skin the animal right after. Microliths allowed them to do this.

The real flexibility of the microlith was its use in combination. These small stones were typically used to form a part of composite tools. These are tools with more than one material or part. The small blades were set in or attached to wood, bone, or antler to

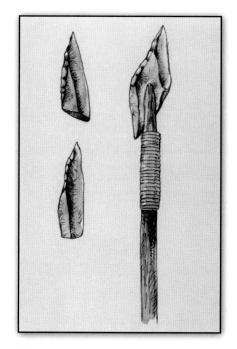

Composite tools were common in the Mesolithic. This composite tool combines two materials, stone and wood.

create tools with handles or with more complex purposes. Composite tools included handles and blades, harpoons, axes, fishing spears, and bows and arrows. Microliths could even be embedded in a curved piece of wood to make a sickle, a curved tool for harvesting plants.

This detachable element of composite tools marked a real advancement in stone technology. The stone could be reworked or replaced when it became worn. Archaeologists have unearthed thrown-away parts of composite stone tools at many Mesolithic sites.

OTHER TOOLS OF THE MESOLITHIC

Microliths were not the only stone tools that people used during the Mesolithic. Larger flake blades could be used for axes. Awls were used to punch holes

THE BOW AND ARROW

The Mesolithic bow and arrow was an example of a composite tool. The bow was often made of wood—such as the trunk of an elm sapling—while the arrowhead was made from stone. The arrowhead could be sharpened to kill the type of prey that the person using it was hunting. Arrows of different shapes and weights could be used to hunt different kinds of prey.

Arrowheads are the sharp tips that are attached to a long shaft to make up an arrow. Since the shafts were generally made of wood—which rots away—few of them have survived. Stone arrowheads are a lot easier to find. In some places, Mesolithic arrowheads have been found in the ground. Other arrows have been found stuck in the remains of animals that were hunted. Barbed arrowheads with sharp bumps suggest something clever about Mesolithic hunters. Such arrowheads may have been used to deliver poison into the hunter's prey.

in animal hides and wood. Scrapers were used to remove fur and fat from animal hides. Grinding tools, such as mortars and pestles, were also used.

The Mesolithic people also became skilled at creating tools that incorporated new plant species. They knotted, twisted, and tied wood, roots, and other plant materials together. Some Mesolithic cultures created

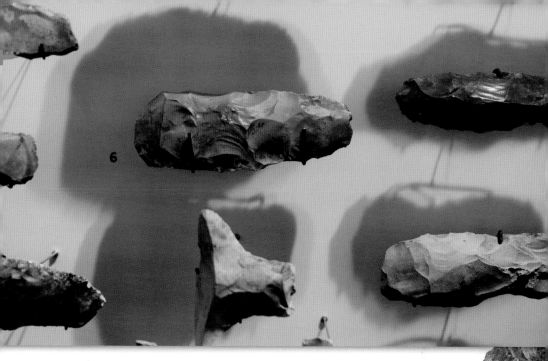

These core axes are from the Maglemosian and Kongemose cultures, which existed in Scandinavia between 8500–5500 BCE.

baskets and fishing nets. They also sewed bags out of birch to carry their flint rock.

The new climate brought people closer to newly formed bodies of water and the fish they provided. Some Mesolithic people wove fishing nets to catch fish. Some made fishing sinks and hooks with microliths. Others used hazel wood rods to form water fences. These fences were likely used to stop fish in their swim path so that they could be easily caught.

BOATS OF THE MESOLITHIC

These new waterways helped give rise to the use and building of boats. Some peoples used boats for

Båden blev padlet frem m
Materialet er hasseltræ
Findested: Ulkestrup i m

This oar, dated to the Mesolithic period in Denmark, shows that Mesolithic peoples were seafaring and making use of the waterways formed after the Ice Age.

fishing. Mesolithic societies tended to form around river valleys and bodies of water. Boats were typically made of wood, which is a material that is not easily preserved. Therefore there are not many remaining boats from the Mesolithic. In some places, though, wooden boats have been preserved in peat bogs and water. For example, Mesolithic dugout boats have been found in Scandinavian bogs. To make these boats, people would hollow out part of a tree trunk with stone axes. Cracks in the wood could be filled with clay or other soft material. Some decorated paddles have been discovered in these areas as well.

Residents of the Nile Valley also used boats. Researchers know this because they have found boat pictures on pebbles dating to the Mesolithic period. They have also used clues to guess at the existence of boats. There is evidence of tools used for fishing in

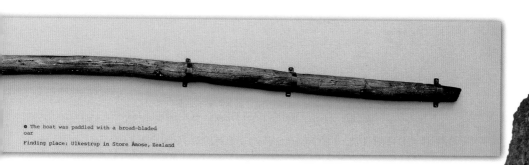

● The boat was paddled with a broad-bladed oar

Finding place: Ulkestrup in Store Åmose, Zealand

the deep water of the Nile. Without boats and rafts, Meso-lithic people would not have been able to reach deep-water fish. There are also islands near England that were occupied by people during the Mesolithic. Without boats people could probably not have reached these islands.

It is likely that the boats that certain Mesolithic soci-eties built made interaction among Mesolithic peoples possible. As people fished along the Atlantic Coast, they may have had more chances to come into contact with other hunter-gatherer bands.

CHAPTER 2
HUNTER-GATHERERS

For most of time that humans have existed, they have been nomadic. They moved around instead of settling in one place. Like most prehistoric people, Mesolithic humans were typically nomadic. Mesolithic people had no grocery stores and no farms to provide them with food. Much of their life was planned around access to food. Mesolithic people lived a hunter-gatherer life. They hunted or caught their food, such as wild land mammals, birds, and fish.

They also gathered or collected plants to eat. Although it is thought that the world's population likely increased in this warmer climate, it appears that they lived in more widespread areas.

Mesolithic peoples lived according to their food sources. Some people in Europe may have traveled north, to follow the reindeer their ancestors had learned to hunt in the Ice Age. Some stayed where they were or dispersed into the woods in search of animals, such as roe deer and wild boar. At least some appear to have settled for parts of the year, taking advantage of the resources in a particular area. In Europe, this was often a clearing in the woods, typically near a source of water, such as a lake. In other places, such as India and the Nile Valley, Mesolithic peoples spent much of their time in locations near rivers, lakes, or seas.

As the old Ice Age animals disappeared, Mesolithic people hunted the new animals they found in the forest such as wild boar, shown here, and red deer.

NATURAL RESOURCES

Many of the animals of the Paleolithic period migrated north or became extinct at the beginning of or during the Mesolithic. Paleolithic peoples had learned to follow and hunt animals that migrated in large herds. The new animals of the forest—such as red deer, elk, and wild boar—were smaller and did not usually live or migrate in large herds. People adapted their hunting skills to kill and capture these animals for food, clothing, and other uses. While there were lots of animals to hunt, the fact that they were smaller and did not live in herds meant that a hunting expedition would provide less meat. This likely pushed Mesolithic people to rely on other resources, beyond land animals, for food.

ICE AGE ANIMALS

The woolly mammoth was a relative of the elephant that lived in cold climates throughout the world. This giant animal weighed several thousand pounds and ate mostly grasses. A warm coat helped it to survive the icy weather. Paleolithic peoples hunted the woolly mammoth for meat. They used its bones and tusks for tools and for artwork. They even built huts with the bones. By the end of the Mesolithic period, these animals were probably completely extinct. The grasses that they once relied on for food no longer grew in the warmer climate. Some scientists now think that hunting by humans contributed to the mammoth's extinction.

With a thick coat and small hooves that spread their weight in snow, reindeer were particularly suited to the Ice Age climate. These animals continued to live in the Mesolithic, but they migrated north and lived in the colder climates. People who remained in the now warm forest learned to hunt their relatives, red deer, and other forest animals.

New coastlines were created as the water from melting glaciers increased sea levels worldwide. This meant increased access to saltwater fish, seals, dolphins, and especially shellfish. Large deposits of shellfish remains have been found at several Mesolithic

This fish is a northern pike. As the ice melted and formed new waterways, Mesolithic peoples had access to fish such as the pike, perch, and shellfish.

sites. Freshwater fish, like pike, also became abundant. Some Mesolithic hunters were expert fishers who used tools such as traps, nets, fishing platforms, and even boats to aid them. Evidence of fishing is found in places such as Scandinavia, the Nile Valley, and Britain. Along these new coastlines, birds formed new migratory routes. Some peoples learned to hunt these sea birds, as well as inland birds.

MESOLITHIC VEGETATION

The changing climate brought a new way of living for the hunter-gatherers. The tundra, which had plants such as grasses, mosses, lichen, and shrubs, turned into a thick, lush forest with a diversity of plant life. The Mesolithic people's diet still included meat but also expanded to depend on the increasing availability of different plant species. Over time, the forests filled with new tree species, such as birch, willow, oak, and elm. Hazelnuts became a very popular food in Europe. Hazel-

Hazelnuts were a good source of nutritious fat during the Mesolithic period. They were also easy for Mesolithic gatherers to transport and store.

nut bushes spread throughout Europe, most likely as the nomadic people carried, ate, and left hazelnuts behind on their travels.

Mesolithic peoples ate the newly available nuts, roots, seeds, fungi, berries, and eventually wild grains. They likely understood where and when to find these plants, as well as which plants could be collected most efficiently. They built tools, such as sickles and grinders, to cut and grind plants into food or fibers for clothes.

TRACING THE MESOLITHIC DIET

Archaeologists must work with whatever remains are left behind. Animal bones and seafood shells are among the items from the Mesolithic period that are most likely to be preserved well over time. However, researchers must look for evidence that is less apparent in order to form a more complete picture.

When plant matter does remain, archaeologists work with botanists. These plant scientists can often date the biological material to tell when the plants originated and determine the plant species. Plants are often not well preserved over time, though. How then do scientists learn more about the diets of Mesolithic peoples? Plants are not preserved well, but bones and teeth are! Archaeologists and scientists study human teeth remains to learn about prehistoric people's diets. The size and shape of teeth tell scientists about the food those teeth chewed. Scientists analyze wear and tear on teeth. Chewing nuts and seeds, such those eaten during the European Mesolithic, can leave behind small, pitted marks on teeth. Chewing softer plants like leaves and fruits can leave behind scratches. After the Mesolithic, changes in human teeth are very apparent. The beginning of farming and processed grains in the Neolithic brought much more tooth decay—and it's never left us!

UNDERSTANDING THEIR HABITAT

Mesolithic hunter-gatherers learned to adapt to their new environment. Mesolithic hunters were experts in their environment. They excelled at understanding and using the natural resources around them. They knew when and where to collect a wide variety of food resources. This meant learning which kinds of mushrooms were safe to eat, what parts of a river were best for fishing in, and where good berry bushes could be found. It also meant knowing when various kinds of fruits were ripe, as well as what the best times of year to harvest nuts or collect shellfish were. It is likely that the Neolithic Revolution built on the skills gained by Mesolithic people's understanding of the animals and plants in their world.

CHAPTER 3
MESOLITHIC LIFE

M uch of the Mesolithic period is still a mystery to archaeologists. The Mesolithic is also a part of what is called prehistory, which refers to time before written language. There are no written stories from this time to tell us what life was like for Mesolithic peoples. There were no photographs or videos yet, and there are far fewer known works of art remaining from the Mesolithic period than the Paleolithic or the Neolithic. The Mesolithic was also many thousands of years shorter than the Paleolithic, so naturally fewer artifacts can be dated to the Mesolithic.

Because of these facts, archaeologists must rely on preserved artifacts, or objects that remain from a past time, to help us picture what Mesolithic life may have been like. They use dating methods such as

Mesolithic peoples likely hunted in groups. Here a group of hunters transport their catch, perhaps back to a temporary settlement near the water.

radiocarbon dating, which measures the amount of carbon 14—a radioactive form of carbon—to determine the age of an object. They look at the art that does remain on rocks, caves, and other surfaces. Archaeologists also use what information we do have about the Mesolithic to make inferences, or reasonable guesses, about the past.

CLOTHING

We have little proof of what Mesolithic people wore. That is because textiles and fabrics are some of the least likely materials to be preserved over time. However, a few artifacts do remain. We can also make guesses about what people wore by looking at rock pictures dated to the Mesolithic period. We can even make some assumptions about what they did not wear yet. Animals were not domesticated until the Neolithic, which means that certain materials would not have been readily available.

Mesolithic people wore skins and furs from the animals they hunted. They likely used tools, such as scrapers, to scrape the fur from hides. Skin pieces were cut, possibly with microliths, and then sewn together loosely. Then people could pierce the skin with awls to make holes. The skins were then tied together, probably with leather ties. Rock art in eastern Spain shows people wearing skirts, pants, and headdresses that were likely made this way.

Mesolithic clothes were likely made from animal hides and plant fibers. Cuts of hides would have been loosely sewn together rather than fitted to the body.

Netting stitched together for fishing nets suggests that some Mesolithic people would have known how to sew with plant fibers. These stitching methods and plant fibers could have also been used to make clothing. Mesolithic people may have taken advantage of the new diversity of plant life to use plant fibers in clothing materials. For example, some Mesolithic people probably wove skirts out of grass. There is good evidence that they wove sleeping mats from rushes. As domesticated sheep did not take hold in most places until the Neolithic, it is unlikely that wool was regularly used to make Mesolithic clothes.

MESOLITHIC SHELTER

One of the more recent developments in Mesolithic research is an understanding of shelter and settlements. Until recently it was thought Mesolithic people were constantly on the go. Any housing that Mesolithic people built was assumed to have been flimsy and portable. This would have been well suited to a nomadic life, in which people needed to pack up and move quickly. Roofs would have been made from hides or branches.

However, recent discoveries have suggested that not all Mesolithic peoples were completely nomadic. Some had

This reconstruction of a Mesolithic hut is near the sea in Scotland. Mesolithic peoples usually chose to live near water. Roofs of temporary huts were probably made of branches.

preferred settlement areas, to which they returned every year on a seasonal basis. People would have planned in advance where to go, based on the season and expected food supply. Evidence of more permanent houses has been unearthed in several places. These were typically open-air settlements (as opposed to settlements in caves, for example) and were located near water. Shelters sometimes had fire pits or hearths for cooking or tool making.

INTERACTION

Mesolithic people typically lived in bands or small family groups. Some Mesolithic peoples also lived and hunted together in larger settlements and groups. Although these groups were likely more widely dispersed than Paleolithic bands had been, there is evidence of interaction between groups of Mesolithic people. Some of these people may have traveled over long distances. In Europe, Mesolithic bands even came together for yearly social gatherings.

In the Balkans, Mesolithic shell necklaces have been found. The shells from which these necklaces were made came from the faraway Black Sea, which suggests a relationship between different hunter-gatherer groups. In other places, there is evidence that the stone used for tools was not available near the area in which the tools were found. This stone traveled long distances, and it may even have

LANGUAGE IN THE MESOLITHIC

Prehistoric peoples developed the use of language thousands of years before the Mesolithic. However, apart from possible symbols for counting, there is no evidence of written language from this time. So researchers must make guesses about what the language spoken by each people was like and how languages were spread during this time.

Several hundred years ago, language experts noticed that there are similarities among many of the languages spoken in Europe, the Middle East, and South Asia. They realized that these languages must be related, so they grouped them together as the Indo-European language family. The family includes languages such as English, French, German, Italian, Greek, Russian, Hindi-Urdu, and Persian. Scholars have determined that all the languages are descended from a single language that existed far in the past, which they call Proto-Indo-European.

Research has suggested that the Neolithic Revolution may have been responsible for the spread of Proto-Indo-European through farming culture or traveling warriors. However, a more recent theory suggests that it was Mesolithic hunter-gatherers who spread the language. Spurred into movement by the changing climate after the Ice Age, they may have carried Proto-Indo-European with them and passed it on to the new people they met as they migrated.

come to an area through trade with other peoples. Some of these trade routes might have involved boat travel.

Late Mesolithic hunter-gatherers and early Neolithic farmers interacted with each other in several places. Although the Neolithic Revolution is considered the time period following the Mesolithic, it took place at different times in different places. It began earlier in the Middle East than in Europe. DNA evidence from human remains suggests both interaction and intermarriage between early Neolithic peoples from the Middle East and Mesolithic Europeans.

In the Balkans, an area in southern Europe, Neolithic farmers and Mesolithic hunter-gatherers likely lived alongside each other by the banks of the Danube River. Mesolithic burial sites there suggest that Mesolithic people incorporated traditions from both hunter-gatherer and farming cultures into their burials. Mesolithic art preserved on boulders with images of creatures that are half-sea animal and half-human is also representative of possible Neolithic influence on Mesolithic communities. In later Mesolithic sites in India, Mesolithic people sometimes used pottery and metal tools. This technology was likely borrowed from nearby Neolithic peoples.

CHAPTER 4
EVIDENCE OF CULTURE: ART AND RELIGION

Art is another tool that archaeologists use to paint a picture of prehistoric times. Where written language does not exist, pictures and other forms of art may help tell a story. This has proven somewhat difficult when studying the Mesolithic, though, since there is less art from that period than from the Paleolithic or Neolithic.

Did most Mesolithic people simply stop making art? Perhaps adapting to life in this new climate required concentrating on survival and left less time for making art. There are, however, other possibilities. Perhaps, the art had not really disappeared, but just changed.

For example, Mesolithic people may have expressed themselves artistically in new ways, working with the new

This stag horn trowel with geometric carvings was made in what is now Italy during the Mesolithic period.

plant fibers and other materials that are unlikely to have survived until the present. A handful of expertly crafted tools and artifacts from the Mesolithic, such as decorated boat paddles, have survived and suggest the beginnings of decorative art.

ROCK ART

During the frozen Paleolithic, people made incredible paintings deep inside caves, whose hidden, dark walls preserved the art from weathering. The few examples of rock painting that have

survived from the Mesolithic period are mostly in shallow caves or on rocks exposed to the open air. It is possible that, because it was exposed, much of the art from this period just didn't survive to the present. Left open to the elements—like wind and rain—rock art on boulders, cliffs, and overhangs may have been worn away.

This rock art in Spain's Cave of the Horses features a hunting scene, a regular element of Mesolithic life.

There are a number of places where Mesolithic rock art has been found. Paintings on exposed rock and in shallow caves appear on Spain's mountainous eastern coast. Unlike Paleolithic cave art, which rarely centered on humans, these pictures show people as important figures. The rock art depicts Mesolithic daily activities such as honey gathering, hunting, warfare, and dancing. These scenes give us a picture of Mesolithic life in southern Europe. Archaeologists use this information to form a picture of how people dressed and how they lived their daily lives.

India, with its extensive rock formations, also has a rich tradition of rock art. At Pachmarhi Hills, in central India, sandstone rock shelters feature rock paintings made in a variety of pigments. These are found throughout the walls and ceilings. The first paintings date to the Mesolithic. The paintings continue until a few hundred years before the present. The Mesolithic pictures here show animals and plants that would be found in the local habitat. Bulls, bison, elephants, fish, peacocks, and other animals are depicted. Human figures are usually shown as hunters.

POTTERY

Archaeologists often study and date prehistoric sites by the pottery they find there, but pottery typically indicates that a site existed after the

Mesolithic. It is usually associated with the Neolithic Revolution. When archaeologists discover pottery at a site, they can often infer that the people lived after the Mesolithic period. There are a few exceptions, though. Pottery has been found in a few Mesolithic sites, in particular those in Khartoum, Sudan.

Why is it that pottery would be associated more with the Neolithic Revolution than the Mesolithic? As people stayed still, living in homes with hearths, they were more likely to make pottery. That is because pottery is made by shaping and then baking clay. It is possible that Mesolithic people knew how to make pottery, too, but did not do so because pottery was not practical for them. Easily breakable pottery may not have been the most useful tool for people living a nomadic life.

RELIGION AND RITUAL

To form an idea of religious and spiritual practices, archaeologists must rely on the information they have from the Paleolithic period to give them an understanding of religious practices that existed already. They also piece together information from the pictures and artifacts of the Mesolithic period. One of the most important sources of information that archaeologists have is burial grounds. Though it is not clear that all Mesolithic people had the same burial traditions, a number of burial grounds with multiple bodies have been found. At burial sites,

These skeletons of a woman and child were found at a Mesolithic site in Denmark. Archaeologists study burial grounds to understand Mesolithic ritual.

archaeologists study human remains but also pay close attention to the locations and positions in which people are buried. They also note whom and what they are buried with. From this information, they infer that Mesolithic peoples valued social relationships and placed some importance on material goods.

Mesolithic peoples were often buried with material goods such as jewelry. Some graves included animal remains, one of the many hints that animals had a

THE STAR CARR HEADDRESSES

Twenty-one red deer skulls with antlers were excavated from the Star Carr site. These skulls, which have holes that may have been tied together with leather pieces, were probably worn as headdresses. This was quite a unique discovery, and much thought has gone into guessing what the skulls were used for. Some people think that hunters wore these headdresses when hunting to disguise themselves as their prey; they saw themselves as part of the natural world. Others argue that the masks were used in ritual shamanistic ceremonies.

special place in Mesolithic spirituality. People were often buried with jewelry made of bone. In some places, people were buried near water. Waterbird remains have been found at burial sites, too. Mesolithic people, like the Paleolithic people before them, may have believed that water was an entrance to the underworld, where the dead lived. Many researchers believe that people of the Paleolithic and Mesolithic periods had a belief system that incorporated shamanism and animism.

Shamanism relies on a person, called a shaman, who links humans to the supernatural world. Mesolithic artifacts point to the possibility that shamanism played a role in Mesolithic life. At the Star Carr site, in England, archaeologists have found a group of deer skulls that were probably worn as headdresses. This find hints at shamanic ritual practice. A nine-thousand-year-old mouth bow made of bone was discovered at a Mesolithic site in Denmark. Since music often plays an important role in modern shamanic ceremonies, it is quite possible that this instrument may have been used by a Mesolithic shaman in a ritual ceremony.

These Mesolithic animal figurines made of amber were found in Denmark. Such charms may have been used in animistic or shamanistic ceremonies.

Animism is the belief that animals and nonhuman natural objects have a soul or supernatural importance. Recent research has suggested that rock itself may have had spiritual meaning for Mesolithic people. Animals certainly played a vital role in Mesolithic life, and animals likely had important spiritual meaning. Hunting was such a crucial part of Mesolithic survival that a bit of bad luck in hunting could mean danger for a band of people. So hunters may have practiced rituals to protect themselves from bad hunting luck. Some Mesolithic people wore charms that were probably intended to protect them during hunting.

Without written language to rely on, descriptions of religion and spirituality in the Mesolithic can only be guesses. It is easy to assume that Mesolithic groups believed in hunting magic, but ritual practice would likely have had different meanings in different places in the world. Without writing to interpret artifacts and images, archaeologists can only make a best guess as to the spiritual beliefs of Mesolithic peoples.

CHAPTER 5

MESOLITHIC ARCHAEOLOGICAL SITES

Archaeologists learn about Mesolithic cultures by conducting excavations in which they dig up materials from the ground or underwater. They study the materials they find and piece together information by comparing it to what they know from other Mesolithic site digs. When large deposits of Mesolithic materials are found, they may signify the existence of larger semipermanent settlements. These are not necessarily representative of how all Mesolithic peoples lived. Still they provide us with valuable information about the time.

STAR CARR

In 1947, John Moore was walking in a field in England when he came upon a flint blade. After this discovery, he found several Mesolithic sites in the area, including Star Carr, an early Mesolithic site. Star Carr is one of the most important Mesolithic sites ever discovered because so many of the artifacts were well preserved. The site's waterlogged peat has helped preserve many artifacts that would otherwise have long since disintegrated.

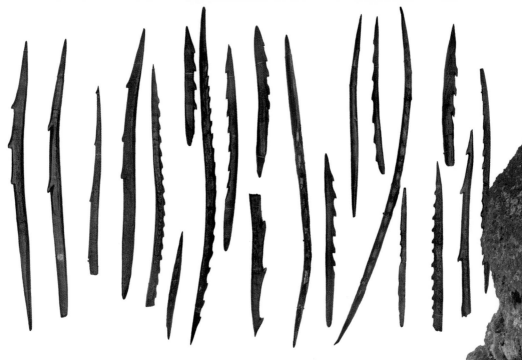

These barbed tools were found at Star Carr. Here, the barbs are located on only one edge and all point away from the point at the top of the tool.

The many artifacts found at Star Carr include micro-liths, axes, and shale jewelry. A lakefront wooden plat-form has also been unearthed. Animal remains include red deer, wild boar, elk, and birds. The site has been excavated several times. Each time more information is unearthed. Most recently, part of a Mesolithic house was discovered. It is the oldest house known in England. Its existence changed the view of how Mesolithic peoples in England lived, suggesting that some Mesolithic peo-ple stayed in one place at least part of the time.

Today Starr Carr is a field, but during the Mesolithic period it was on the edge of a lake and its residents made use of a long lakefront platform. Starr Carr would have been a beautiful place to live, and it's no wonder that people probably chose to return there repeatedly. Initially archaeologists guessed that Star Carr was home to no more than a few families, but now they believe it was probably a much larger thriving seasonal settlement.

Researchers continue to study and write about Star Carr. In recent years, an excavation was conducted because researchers feared that the peat drying up would no longer preserve the site's remaining artifacts if they waited too long.

MESOLITHIC KHARTOUM

During World War II, people made an important find during construction at a hospital site in Khartoum. Khartoum is a city in Sudan, an African country bordering Egypt. The city sits at the intersection of the Blue Nile and White Nile, which flow into the Nile River. Artifacts were unearthed that led to the discovery of a Mesolithic culture in the area that is now Khartoum. Other sites were discovered nearby after this initial find at the hospital site.

The people of Mesolithic Khartoum lived between 8000 and 4000 BCE. The Khartoum hospital site may have been inhabited seasonally for as long as a few thousand years. These hunter-gatherers may have been semi-sedentary, having found a hospitable site to live along on the Nile for part of the year. Every

Archaeological Digs

An archaeological dig is also called an excavation. Sometimes digs are begun after someone happens upon an artifact. That person shares it with researchers who will want to learn everything they can about the material. Before conducting a dig, archaeologists will do research on the period they are studying. Archaeologists of prehistory like the Mesolithic work by digging up and studying artifacts to learn about the time from which they came. Archaeologists conducting a dig don't wear suits to work. They need to be prepared to dig in the soil.

Archaeologists excavate sites in layers. They dig up materials such as stone tools, architectural features, plant matter, animal bones, and even human remains. Sometimes, a particular site will include a range of prehistoric and historic evidence. The strata, or layers, in which materials are found help the archaeologists date the materials. Newer materials are usually in the top layers. The layers below are increasingly older. For example, Neolithic layers will likely be found above the Mesolithic layers, while Mesolithic ones will be above Paleolithic ones. Sometimes prior to digging a natural event such as an earthquake may have shifted the layers.

Diggers try to dig sideways instead of making holes, which helps preserve evidence. Archaeologists sometimes set up a rope grid over the area being excavated. This helps them keep track of where they are digging. The diggers take care to note how the materials are positioned when they are found. After the dig, they may work with other researchers like botanists, paleontologists, and art historians to study the materials they have found.

year, when the Nile River flooded the land, the people probably left to live in the nearby desert or plains. In the winter they returned to fish in the Nile.

The excavators at the hospital site found buffalo, porcupine, hippopotamus, crocodile, and snail remains. The people of Mesolithic Khartoum most likely survived by hunting animals and fishing in the river, where they caught fish and river snails. They also likely gathered wild grains and fruit.

Hippopotamus bones are one of the many types of animal bones found at the hospital site in Khartoum, near the Nile River.

One material that sets Khartoum apart from other Mesolithic sites is pottery, which does not appear in most other places until the Neolithic Revolution. These clay pots were decorated with wavy lines that were possibly formed using catfish bone before the clay dried.

Other artifacts found at the site include barbed spears, microliths made of quartz pebbles, and grinding stones. The grinding stones may have been used to grind wild grain and red ocher. Ocher is a natural pigment made from rock. The people of Mesolithic Khartoum may have used it to decorate pottery and for face painting. There are also formal burial remains at the Khartoum hospital site, with offerings at the graves.

BAGOR

From 1968 to 1970, an excavation was carried out at one of the largest Mesolithic sites ever found in India. This was the first Indian Mesolithic site to be dug horizontally, or with sidewise digging, which helped preserve the site. The Mesolithic layer at Bagor is waterlogged. This kept an unusual number of artifacts well preserved over time.

Bagor is on the bank of the Kothari River in the Rajasthan region of India. Here, people likely lived semi-sedentary lives, returning to the settlement at Bagor seasonally. The shelters had floors paved with stone slabs and pebbles. Paving stones were probably brought across the river. The upper parts of the shelters were likely made from wood or other plant matter.

One of the key features at Bagor is a large group of tiny geo-metrically shaped microliths. These tools are a bit of a mystery. Some of the microliths at Bagor are so small that they are diffi-cult to hold in the hand. Hammerstones have also been found at the site. These were likely used for splitting animal bones. There is also evidence of stone slabs used for butchering.

The people at Bagor likely relied on a mix of fishing, harvest-ing grains, and hunting to survive. However, some researchers believe that animal remains in the Mesolithic layer include sheep bones. This fact is in dispute now, as it is not easy to tell if these are really the bones of sheep or other, wild animals. If the bones belonged to sheep, then the Bagor would have been a particularly unusual group, already raising and herding animals in the Mesolithic period.

The practice of domesticating sheep may have been introduced by Neolithic farmers with whom the Bagor people certainly had contact. One reason archaeologists know this is that they have found copper arrowheads dated to the Mesolithic period at Bagor, an unusual find for a Stone Age site. This knowledge would have come from Neolithic communities in which people knew how to work with metal.

UNDERWATER MESOLITHIC

Archaeologists continue to locate new Mesolithic sites. These add to our changing picture of the Meso-lithic period. One source of new Mesolithic discoveries

The North Sea now covers Doggerland, which once connected Britain to continental Europe.

lies underwater. As the oceans continued to rise during the Mesolithic, they covered areas that had been dry land. One place where this happened was Doggerland.

Doggerland was once a land bridge between Scotland and Denmark. It connected Britain to the mainland of Europe. It now lies underneath the North Sea. Scientists once thought that Doggerland was not of much importance and that few people lived there, but they now believe it was a very important part of Mesolithic Europe where many hunter-gatherers lived. Finds of underwater artifacts combined with the creation of underwater geological maps have helped scientists to make a picture of Mesolithic Doggerland. They believe it was a thriving and hospitable location for hunter-gatherers, who were forced to leave as the waters rose up over the land.

CHAPTER 6
THE END OF
THE MESOLITHIC

Mesolithic peoples were hunter-gatherers who were nomadic at least much of the time. The Neolithic Revolution changed much of human culture. Instead of searching for their food and useful natural resources, humans became food producers. At one time, researchers saw this as a rapid shift, but that viewpoint has changed as they learn more about the Mesolithic period. It is likely that this shift built on the skills people learned in the Mesolithic period. Mesolithic hunter-gathers gained a deep knowledge of the plants and animals in a newly biodiverse world.

It now seems that many Mesolithic people did more than exploit their environment by gathering existing plants and hunting animals. They were also manipulating the land and environment both intentionally and unintentionally. Some of these manipulations may have brought about the transition to the Neolithic period. It is possible, for example, that overharvesting may have decreased the population of shellfish in certain areas, creating a reason for humans to produce their own food. It also seems likely that some Mesolithic people scattered seeds and planted roots to grow. Others may have diverted water to help plants grow. This knowledge about plant growth would have been beneficial for farming in the Neolithic period.

At the same time, Mesolithic peoples were also cutting down trees to build shelter, boats, and tools with wood. They formed walking paths through trees and plants that likely continued to serve as pathways in the Neolithic.

MANAGEMENT BY FIRE

One key way that some Mesolithic people managed their environment was through fire. Some Mesolithic peoples in continental Europe and England likely used fire to clear trees, which may have helped new plants such as hazelnuts, crabapples, and berries grow. The fire did more than spur new plant growth. It provided clearings in the wilderness for humans to make settlements. Fire as a land-management tool likely increased in the Neolithic when people needed to clear land for crops and for animal grazing.

ANIMAL DOMESTICATION

These clearings may have also attracted particular prey, such as red deer. Mesolithic peoples may have intentionally killed predator animals so as to leave preferred animals for human hunting. Mesolithic people may have begun capturing and raising animals rather than waiting to find them in the wild. These factors helped begin animal domestication, which is how humans breed animals for desired traits, such as size. The clearings likely contributed to early animal herding.

THE DOG

Animal domestication is usually a marker of the Neolithic period. However Mesolithic peoples were beginning to domesticate animals. The best example is probably the dog. The remains of domesticated dogs have been found in widespread Mesolithic sites.

The first dogs were likely bred in Asia. Until recently, scientists believed that dogs were first domesticated in Europe at the beginning of or just prior to the beginning of the Mesolithic period. But new remains suggest they may have been around much longer than that, possibly forty thousand years before, in the Paleolithic.

Wolves are the closest wild relation of dogs. Unlike animals that were domesticated later, dogs were probably not domesticated for food. Scientists have different ideas about how they were domesticated. One idea is that hunter-gatherer groups may have taken in babies as pets, who then grew used to living near humans.

Dog remains have been found at Mesolithic sites in places such as England, Portugal, Scandinavia, Ireland, and India. They were sometimes buried with humans, suggesting an important relationship between dogs and people. In some cases dogs were given special burials. Dogs are thought to have assisted Mesolithic people in hunting, but more importantly served as companions, just as they do for people today.

This gray wolf is a close relative of the dog. Mesolithic peoples appear to have domesticated their neighbor wolves into the dog companions we know today.

There is evidence that Mesolithic people in Germany already had domesticated pigs, possibly gained through contact with Neolithic groups from the Middle East. The people of Mesolithic Khartoum may have domesticated sheep prior to the Neolithic Revolution. Mesolithic excavation sites reveal the presence of domesticated dogs on different continents.

THE NATUFIAN

The Natufian culture came into being around fourteen thousand years ago in the Levant, or eastern Mediterranean region. The people of this culture did something unusual for the time. They stopped wandering

and stayed in one place throughout the year.

What made this group of people decide to settle while other Middle Eastern peoples were still living nomadic lives? Perhaps there was simply enough food to eat in one spot that they could stay there without moving. Perhaps they stayed to spend more energy cultivating the wild grains around them. The grinding tools and sickles found on Natufian sites

This Natufian grinding tool made from limestone was likely used to grind grains for food.

suggest extensive harvesting and processing of grains. The Levant at this time also had ample animals to hunt, such as birds, gazelle, and fish. Whatever the reason, the Natufians apparently chose to stay, at least for a time.

Archaeologists determined that the Natufians were mostly sedentary based on the structures they built. Natufian sites have more extensive architecture than other Mesolithic sites. They resemble early villages. Natufian houses were built partly underground, with bottoms made of stone. The upper portion was likely made of wood. Evidence of underground storage sites for grain has been found, suggesting seasonal planning. Above ground, people likely stored grains in baskets. Archaeologists have also found evidence of mice and house sparrows, which are animals that live in places where humans settle.

In addition to artifacts such as stone tools and bowls, the Natufians also left behind far more extensive artwork than other cultures of the time. Animal figurines, pottery, and decorated ostrich egg containers have been found at Natufian sites. At burial sites, archaeologists have found jewelry expertly crafted from bone, shell, and stone.

TRANSITION

The Natufians' settled village life, extensive artwork, and storage of grain were traits of the coming Neolithic period in the Middle East. Perhaps this was a natural end to the time that Mesolithic peoples had spent learning about the plants and animals in their environment.

Yet farming, at least at first, was not such an easy way of life. Whereas hunter-gatherers could move to find food sources, farmers were dependent on the food they were able to grow. Some researchers think Mesolithic peoples in the Middle East and Europe turned to farming out of necessity. Climate change may have brought a drier environment to the Levant and decreased the local food supply. Perhaps the nearby food resources had been overexploited, and a population increase also meant increase in competition for land and food resources. Some Mesolithic peoples appear to have turned to violence toward each other in this competitive world. Perhaps, too, although farming itself was difficult, living in a community in one place seemed like a more enjoyable way of life.

Mesolithic people harvested wild grains, but Neolithic people learned to grow them.

THE NEOLITHIC REVOLUTION

The Neolithic Revolution would spread east into India and west into southern Europe and then northern Europe. Researchers do not agree, though, on how the spread was achieved. Did Neolithic warriors conquer Mesolithic hunger-gatherers? Perhaps Mesolithic peoples saw opportunity for material wealth with the ability to domesticate animals and cultivate plants. Maybe it was a little of each.

We may never know, but what is clear is that from this time forward most people would devote their lives to food production, relying on domesticating, raising, and herding animals and growing their own crops. There are still nomadic peoples and hunter-gathers today, but mostly we live in a world of settled communities, whether that means villages, cities, or something in between. Until the end of the Mesolithic period, most people of the world were nomadic. At the end of the Mesolithic, people decided to stop moving. Civilization was about to begin.

TIMELINE

12,500–10,200 BCE Natufian culture exists in the eastern Mediterranean.

12,500 BCE The Mesolithic period begins in Denmark.

11,600 BCE The Ice Age ends in Europe.

10,000 BCE The Mesolithic period begins in Britain.

10,000 BCE The Neolithic period begins in the Middle East.

9000 BCE The Mesolithic period beings in India.

8700 BCE Beginning of occupation at Star Carr in Britain.

8000 BCE Doggerland is abandoned as it is submerged by the North Sea.

8000–4000 BCE Khartoum Mesolithic culture exists in what is now Sudan.

8000 BCE Mesolithic rock art is created in eastern Spain.

4000 BCE The Neolithic period begins in northern Europe.

1944 CE Mesolithic artifacts are discovered at Khartoum hospital site in Sudan.

1947 CE The Star Carr settlement site is discovered in Britain.

1968 CE Excavation begins at Bagor.

2013 CE Britain's oldest house is discovered at Star Carr.

2015 CE Archaeologists at University of Bradford, in England, announce plans for major exploration and mapping of Doggerland.

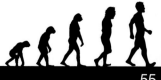

GLOSSARY

animism The belief that nonhuman animals, plants, or objects found in nature have supernatural or spiritual meaning.

artifact An object or material that serves as evidence from a previous time and is often studied by archaeologists to learn about the time.

biodiverse Having a wide variety of different kinds of plants and animals.

composite Made of multiple parts.

domesticate To breed animals or plants for desired traits.

efficiently Quickly and with the least amount of work.

excavation An archaeological dig.

hearth An area that has been prepared for lighting a fire for warmth or cooking.

hunter-gatherer A person who survives by hunting or catching animals and collecting plants for food.

manipulating Controlling or changing for a desired result.

microlith A tiny stone tool, often made of flint and found in large numbers at Mesolithic sites. Microliths were often used to make composite tools.

Neolithic period The late Stone Age, during which people settled in permanent communities, depended on farming for food, and used more polished stone tools than they had in the past.

nomadic Living a wandering life or moving around.

overexploited Used too much, to the point of using up.

Paleolithic period The early Stone Age, during which people
were nomadic and used large, rough stone tools.
retreated Moved back, or left, often out of necessity or fear.
sedentary Not moving; staying in one place.
shamanism A practice in which a human shaman serves as
a go-between for people and the supernatural world.
submerge To cover with something, usually water.
thriving Successful, healthy, and abundant.
unearthed Found or discovered, usually by digging up.

FOR MORE INFORMATION

Canadian Archaeological Association
Lisa Rankin, Department of Archaeology
Memorial University
St. John's, NL A2C 5S7
Canada
Website: http://canadianarchaeology.com/caa
The Canadian Archaeological Association is dedicating to sharing
   archaeological research and promoting archaeology throughout
   Canada.

The Field Museum
1400 S. Lake Shore Drive
Chicago, IL 60605
(312) 922-9410
Website: https://www.fieldmuseum.org
The Field Museum is devoted to teaching about the sciences, including archaeology and anthropology. The museum's archaeologists
   contribute to excavations around the world.

The Milwaukee Public Museum
800 West Wells Street
Milwaukee, WI 53233
(414) 278-2794
Website: http://www.mpm.edu
The Milwaukee Public Museum is a museum of human and
   natural history. Visitors to the museum and the website can
   view examples of Mesolithic stone tools from Scandinavia.

The Royal Ontario Museum
100 Queen's Park
Toronto, ON M5S 2C6
Canada
(416) 586-8000
Website: http://www.rom.on.ca/en
The Royal Ontario Museum is devoted to natural history and
culture. Archaeologists from the museum participate in excavations worldwide, and the museum's collections feature
thousands of artifacts, including Stone Age tools.

The Stone Age Institute
P.O. Box 5097
Bloomington, IN 47407
(812) 876-0080
Website: www.stoneageinstitute.org
The Stone Age Institute is a research center devoted to
advancing studies in archaeology and human evolution.
One of the institute's projects is to create songs about
human evolution and archaeological artifacts.

WEBSITES

Because of the changing nature of Internet links,
Rosen Publishing has developed an online list of
websites related to the subject of this book. This site is
updated regularly. Please use this link to access the list:

http://www.rosenlinks.com/FHEC/meso

For Further Reading

Brooks, Beatrice D., and Carvalho De Magalhaes. *Art and Culture of the Prehistoric World*. New York, NY: Rosen Central, 2010.

Brooks, Philip. *The Story of Prehistoric Peoples*. New York, NY: Rosen Central, 2013.

Butterfield, Moira. *The Stone Age* (Britain in the Past). London, England: Franklin Watts, 2015.

Farndong, John. *100 Things You Should Know About Archaeology*. Broomall, PA: Mason Crest Publishers, 2010.

Frith, Alex. *Prehistoric Britain*. London, England: Usborne Books, 2015.

Green, Jan. *The Stone Age and Bronze Age: Discover Through Craft*. London, England: Franklin Watts, 2015.

Hattstein, Marcus. *Prehistory, First Empires, and the Ancient World: From the Stone Age to 900 CE* (Witness to History: A Visual Chronicle of the World). New York, NY: Rosen Classroom, 2012.

Hibbert, Clare. *The History Detective Investigates: Stone Age to Iron Age*. London, England: Wayland, 2014.

Hurdman, Charlotte. *Hands on History: The Stone Age*. Durham, NC: Armadillo Books, 2014.

Newland, Sonya. *Stone, Bronze, and Iron Ages* (Explore!). London, England: Wayland, 2015.

Steele, Kathryn. *Stones and Bones: Archaeology in Action*. New York, NY: Rosen Publishing, 2013.

BIBLIOGRAPHY

Adams, Jonathan, and Marcel Otte. "Did Indo-European Languages Spread Before Farming?" *Current Anthropology* 40 (1999): 73–77.

Arkell, Anthony John. "The Excavation of an Ancient Site at Khartoum," *Sudan Notes and Records* 25 (1945): 329–331.

Bar-Yosef, Ofer. "The Natufian Culture in the Levant, Threshold to the Origins of Agriculture," *Evolutionary Anthropology* 6 (1998): 159–177.

Coneller, Chantal. "The Mesolithic," in *The Oxford Handbook of the Archaeology of Ritual and Religion*. Timothy Insoll, ed. New York, NY: Oxford University Press, 2012.

Cunliffe, Barry. *The Oxford Illustrated History of Prehistoric Europe*. Oxford, UK: Oxford University Press, 1994.

Misra, Virendra Nath. "Bagor—A Late Mesolithic Settlement in North-west India," *World Archaeology* 5 (1973) 92–110. (http://www.jstor.org/stable/124156).

Mithen, Steven. *After the Ice: a Global Human History, 20,000–5,000 BC*. London, England: Weidenfeld & Nicolson, 2003.

National Museum of Denmark. "Prehistoric Period (until 1050 AD) /The Mesolithic Period." (http://en.natmus.dk).

Star Carr Archaeology Project. "History of Research." (https://sites.google.com/site/starcarrfieldwork/history-of-research).

Tedesco, Laura Anne. "Pachmari Hills (ca. 9000–3000 B.C.)." Metropolitan Museum of Art, October 2000 (http://www.metmuseum.org/toah/hd/pach/hd_pach.htm).

INDEX

ABOUT THE AUTHOR

Lori Fromowitz is a writer and practicing speech-language pathologist. She earned her B.A. in theater from Bard College, where she studied playwriting, and holds an M.S. in communication sciences and disorders. Lori is the author of four previously published nonfiction books for young readers. She currently lives in Massachusetts.

PHOTO CREDITS

Designer: Matt Cauli; Editor: Amelie von Zumbusch; Photo Researcher: Bruce Donnola